EVERYTHING IS NECESSARY

poe

KEISHA-GAYE ANDERSON

WILLOW BOOKS

Detroit, Michigan

Everything Is Necessary

Editor: Randall Horton

Author photo: Rachel Eliza Griffiths
Background art: Keisha-Gaye Anderson
Cover art: B. Robinson
Cover design: Cristina Castro Pelka

ISBN 978-1-7322091-2-1
LCCN 2019932401

Willow Books, a Division of Aquarius Press
www.WillowLit.net

For my children, my teachers—Marcus and Maya—
who have always traveled with me.

Contents

Dark of Moon

Dark of moon
night
baptized by cold sweat and
my heart
beats out
a name
I remember
only from the
black
no-thing
encircling the night sky
behind my eyes

This song
sounds like "mother"
before the Atlantic covered
her
and left me half blind

Where are you, Mami?

Can you help me see
through this morass?

Pull the anchor of speech
from behind my tongue
and tune me to
the melody
that pushes mist up
to sky

Won't you exhale
and send the tides
to carry me
off this strange bridge
between walking bodies
and sleeping souls?

7

No.

And she rocks me
with her words
spoken by my voice:

No one is going to help you
do what you want to do,
little one

Keep going.

Where Are the Soldiers?

Where are my brothers
to brace me
against these torrents of shattered glass
that bury our past
before cane and breeding
name this body according to its yielding
and bend love backward into hate
because the swarm cannot
take the Earth's heartbeat?

No electric embrace
No battle hymn serenade
No midnight map passed
between perfumed breath
No rest
on this journey
a road cleared only by
machete tongue
strong backs
and three eyes

We arrive
each season
scraping through the dark
to quiet our screaming blood
echoes of bodies broken
in our making
solely for the taking
of this blue fire
now damned to ditches
where we consume ourselves
push up plumes
of liquor breath
collect Lotto tickets
pop pills to silence every

djembé drum ripple
whispering to us
from the edge of the
rainbow

But we know that this
frigid air circling our confusion
flickering lights in rooms
of seclusion
are love letters
from all the muted voices
rattling this mind
with pleas insistent
and piercing
jagged bones
in the abyss
of the Atlantic

And they become my eyes
strangers' eyes in every mirror
making me long to know
who speaks this mouth today
who talks behind the curtain of sleep
to say

Remember
Remember
Remember

But I only wade into slumber
and wake to face
the cold
feed the mouths
stay alive

How long do I have to
armor my heart
walk both sides
prop up my pride

and give everybody
everything that I am?

Where are the soldiers?

Refugee

I stand before you
as a refugee
casualty of war

I don't know if my
mother's
mothers'
mothers
were conceived out of love or entitlement

I just know that I am here

And I have walked every mile of this journey in honesty
pulling them with me
like a parachute
brandishing the badges of their faces
in liars' dens

Chanting my
father's
fathers'
fathers
indignation as a spell for protection
scribing the music of their
bravery onto lanterns
called poetry

And it often hurts,
this awareness
scorching the path
that carried you
here
in the echo of
voices
shrieking
sinking into
bewilderment

cemented as fragments
of discontent
in your blood
a war spelled like your name

But there is only
one way out of this
confusion
this circular story
that fabricates
your character
programs the details
of your mission
and the rhythm
of your satiety
and suffering
into placenta

We must climb
until it burns
up that rope
of knotted name
and kin
and shame
that brands
our limbs
with the obscenity
of this reality

And stare the snake
right between the eyes

Dance in the mirror
that shows ugly
and pretty
as one shape
melt the chains clanking around
your mind
into a sword or

a whip or
a lasso
and start an inferno
that burns the whole house
down

Know the sound
that comes through you
as voice
is just one note
in the chant
broadcast
from the throats
of them who sent you forth
and are now calling you
home

Know that
it's safe there
in that sole somewhere
and that you can stop
running
start knowing
how and why
you matter
scan scope of the grid
and conspire to collapse it

No more running
through this
we command this
body be a castle
for our vision
a doorway
to our corona
where every color
shape
thought
conceived

unfolds from us
seeds

Stand still and
see
how we be
limitless

At Some Time Ago

At some time
ago
in this family tree
there was
loving peace
laughter
safety
in wide open
ground and sky
there was
no prey on
two feet
en masse
souls traded for
cash
there was
deep deep sleep
dipping
when we pleased
into an ocean story
of those gone home
and when visiting was done,
there was stretching toward the sun
mango sweetness
ocean salt lips
cosmos cool skin
love making
from toes to nape
there was
no weight like drapes
lain across the fire of your mind
where you run through a maze
of numbness
trying to keep ablaze
the spark
and why even that?

Just to be a lantern for your
kin
as they walk the dark
pulled by husks
around this worm-eaten carousel

What curse is this, mother?
Where do we untie it?

Ancestors

You wanted to look
into the dark
didn't you?

So, don't curse these eyes
We gave them to you

And sent you to
straighten the bends in
these steel tracks
that link all of our names
rusted under salt water
buried beneath bundles
of cane

Sing songs into candle flame
for these bones of mine
that now reach through you
stand you into
six feet of woman

They have not forgotten how to
brace against the lash
and bend backward
for the bembé

Each day
we move with you
Can't you hear?
We are riding the rhythm
that beats these words
through your center

You beg us to enter
but we never left
We is me
is you

is us
all now
together
since forever

We laugh
and lift
your sight toward
starshine
seashells
sleeping poetry
in every alley
and pissed on corner

We tune your ears
to the footfall of predators
who stroke their loneliness
to the bow line of your lips

You wanted to know
not believe
so see it all here
now

And build a ladder
with these visions
that lift us up
one by one
hand over hand
afterbirth
to under dirt

We listen with you
roll slow up
this mountain
that needed us to
tumble down
break ground
move things

So, look here—
kill your fear
open these eyes
pull us back together
march us home

I Remember Forgetting

I probably
forgot
that I came here
to forget
and have spent my
life
trying to remember
spinning
through cycles
of personality
retracing my steps
failing in the same ways
over and over
again
but to taste honey
or my lover's
tongue
to scratch an itch
or dip bread
in gravy
and swallow it
feel the lump
slide down my
throat
makes it worth
all the work

Vital Statistics

Country of origin:

                Orphan

Race:

                Survival Mode

Address:

                The Margins

Date of birth:

                Sea/Sphere
                in here/out there

                same thing

Occupation:

                Masquerader
                or
                Placater
                or
                Pacifier
                or
                Caretaker of Liars

Hair lies sedated for jobs created for those living in

                                    shallow graves

Today's date:

                Overdue

Have you ever been arrested of convicted of

                        Seeing without blinking?
                            Talking the truth?
                                Tracing the lines
                            of the puzzle

                                    With your cut-eye
                        and steuppps?

Watch di fool dem
rats in the maze
Can you eat money?
Can you finance more days?

Excuse me, m'am, are you listening?
Aren't you hungry?
Do you want to get paid?

Sign your name
here
and we'll ration
your stay

Strange Food

I've swallowed my pride
so many times,
the words have
burned a hole
in me
churned themselves
into a bilious chant
that can only
conjure me
into a huddle
with my shadow
at the altar of this self
demanding answers
to the question
that sculpted this face
this time
and sent it into
my husband's 13 year-old
dreams
13 years between him
and me
he was expecting me
I was expecting to be
free
of questions
have acuity of vision
excavate a way home
within
but instead
I play a dull role
in dim light
for a meal
for safe negro
credentials
so my children will be
spared
the firing range

it's a strange state,
silent mouth
swallowing acid
but we've been devouring
ourselves since
since there were
things to
buy and sell
since the world's
stubborn solidity
still, I will
use my tongue
to lick myself on fire
clean off the soot
of sight in 2D
do whatever it
takes to find
the navigator of
this body
and beg her
to wake up

Somnambulism

This somnambulism
life in objects
riding the rapids of currency
gorging on a daily glut of screens
that train sight to shrink
hypnotizes
scatters me,
severed from
the cause
now, so distant,
I can't recall
my descent into this bramble
a circuit of drills
for a war
drawn into my skin
I need a different kind
of being
above the rainbow
under the well spring
within every drop of
warm ocean mist
I miss the knowing
that can see through
any shape
and still remember its way
back home
fold effortlessly into the music
that makes mountains
and orchids
holds the fullness
of black night
in place
so that we may
at once
go in
feel the grandeur
of the whole

of stillness
of being
of the point
of performance
that moves across
the grid
through years
and voices
just to find a mirror
and remember
yes,
I am everything
and I am
enough

Kalunga

The space is thick
with voices
life force
spinning through unknown corridors
of your mind

You always feel
the happy in a room
and the loss
it presses on your chest
the weight of a collapsed
star

This is the vocation of your
skin
daughter of seers
on the indigo road
who seek to temper
you in this place
turn you into a
hearth for
the stolen children

One day you will swim
these waters with ease
without drowning
or gasping in the riptide
of resentment

One morning
you will emerge
through the bottom
of the ocean
and be free

Echo

Back pain came with me
from a life half remembered
the aching echo
of something splintered and lost
begging to be loved today

Letter from Home

Don't get lost
in the words
just know what we did
in fetid cabins
of cane cutters
and secret priests
where we chanted
you a talisman
for your turn
on our long journey
Feel it in the legs
that carry you forward
the mouth we use
to speak through your
voice
the ropes of your crown
that reach for the sun
the sheath of
your golden skin
The only map you ever need
are the pieces of us
in the shape of your face
the you that
is
right now

Walking the Circle

How many times
can you walk a circle?

You are breathless
in this
flesh
blind and forgetful
and partially deaf
pulled by the nose
across the globe like cattle
aching from a boundless hunger
which is really only
questions

Why I?
Why now?
Why pain?
Why at all?

And you are marching
toward
that carrot
straight into the mouths
of cannibals
who live in your
peripheral vision
in the foreground
in the background
in the space in
between your eyes

They are a mist
coating you with
a mask that you
mistake for
your reflection

So when you hear,

A man was shot today
A boy was lynched today
A street vendor was bulldozed today
A woman was raped today
A child...

You say,
"That is them"

But
how many times can you walk a circle
And not
know that

You are the corpse
The strange fruit
The wrinkled street vendor
The woman sawed in two
The child
The child
The child?

How many times
how fast
can you walk
a circle
before crashing into
yourself?

Pendulum

They say
love and hate
are the same thing,
only differing by degrees
but what does that mean for
me?

A pendulum
is no kinda place
to live
rolling in mud in the morning
and starch/bleached
clean at night
I'm looking for the hand
that's swinging my world
set me in motion
poured me into skin
so I could scale
the sinking ladder
of emotion
0 to 10
and back to 0
again

Maybe I'll just
stop climbing
stay still
stargaze
laugh
dream
taste
play
in the center
of this kaleidoscope
until I become
an entirely different
question

Meditation

me is
there
no you
is here no
us is where
space
dissipates into
music
called body
nimbus clouds
tulip crowns
dancing breath
in my chest
and I see your doves
all around me
is you
is us
and now
I hear your
love songs
in the mouths of
passers by
is you
is us
is and I am me
because you look
through my eyes
see me
speak me
into you
is me
is us
is now
is always
love

Knowing

Start from the
knowing
that a man is just
a microphone
another shape
singing the grace
of the creator
and see that
you can talk
the story
falling before your
very own eyes
in perfect
key

"Any stone can
sing"

Let words thunder
shatter lying screens
twisting colors
that hypnotize
numb the hum
of heart
damn the life
that moves this body
across the canvass
of reality

Streak the world
with new colors
and scare them awake
don't let the mirage
break you in two

God is no
where

God is
you

Live Louder

I am a controlled explosion

prisoner of war
bred to be half a memory
of conjure
rhythm
and myth
with one foot fastened
in progress
but only deep enough to
tether us
to the spaces they place
all our mothers
      lifters
              scrubbers
                     diggers
     lovers
             sowers
    seers
             pacifiers
                         breeders
chanters of praise songs
hidden in lullabies
especially for when the storm winds blow high—
Hail
     bullets
Lightning
     tasers
Muddy soil
     every bleeding body
           of murdered
                black boys

And when we start to
overstand that up is
down
trace the grid

with our laughter
through
dream
drum
and trance

When we begin
to hear the rattling
insistence
of salt bones
marking the way
of this route
that could only end
with us
right here
right now

Then the ones who lay
brick over forest
and weld their lives
to trinkets
beg us
to release the
battalion of our voices
but only if the words
are strapped to a bit
as we haul
the republic toward
its next conquest

They want
rote recitation of
the same old
script
so that the sufferers
stand still
sit and
wait
don't hate

this cage
just pray
for heaven
it won't come today
but soon
and very soon
the lord is coming
there's no use running

But there is
one thing
they should know:

My damned body
is bursting with memory
is a library
that has been burned
so many times
the ash runs
through my veins
is a river story
cycling through lives
etching our faces on
stone in every anywhere
that be

And water has always been
free
go where it
will
seek its own embrace
gather the memories
leave the debris
so that we can see
as we pass through
this hall of mirrors
that projects shapes
making industry
look noble

molds us all into
cogs
mops
hammers
wrenches
respectable
receptacles
for square things
built by children
digging up the earth
in search of
their father's faces
and finding only ours

We must know
in this time
that their names and spaces for us
these categories
filed between legal tender
and concrete
broadcast in handcuffed teens
on screens
are a deceit with an
expiration date

We be more like
the ocean
holding the world in place
sending shapes up
into this habitat
for even the dimmest light
to learn the faces
of creation

We are done with patience
if they cannot learn
the most obvious truth
sitting inside a grain of
corn

wrapped in breath
rushing
through our chests
then we will lift ourselves
into a tsunami
and wash the lies
from sight
summon the sea of spirit
scaffolding these bodies
to raise the doorway
out of
this nightmare
where clay tries to
lasso the stars
because they
do not understand
our birthright
cannot see with such
small eyes

Truly,
we know no death
we only forget
lend ourselves to this story
to add chapters
play the parts
that help to grow
greater questions
but we cannot rest here

The dead cannot
hold us
force cannot control
us

when we decide
when we accept
that we are

free
are now
are as it's ever
been
a single moment
flowing out
from one idea

We can no longer doubt
what sits inside ourselves
and watches
it does not know never
or fear
or can't
it only grows out
from where we stand

So stand sure
in the center
of this
all
we did not fall
without
a net
without an army riding
on the waterfall
of slumber
whispering the way forward
as we wander

Our crowns
are already paid for
our names
are already
written on
tomorrow
so incinerate sorrow

Live
louder

Peephole

While I peer
through this peephole
a face dropped into
time
for an exercise in
expansion

I/will
create a ruckus
with these redwood
limbs
pour cold verse
into ears of
sleeping
queens
hiding under tresses
shorn for the goddess

I/will
make love non-stop
'till the body drops
so the Spirit
can step into my men
lift them
into flight
forward like the Trade Winds

I/will play mas
as someone playing
me
so my
daughters can finally say
yes to every inch of flesh
that surrounds them
and know the shape
that caused every other shape
to be

44

I/will watch you
watching me
to make sure you are really
seeing
when you look
and even when I retire
from this point of view
if you close your eyes
call my name
I'll still be with
you

Relay

I'ma run the hell outta this relay
soul stride
Earth stint
slow sprint
bone prison
life mission
to leave memory
as a compass
thin the veil
end the time

And I will move
toward the horizon
lead my daughters to the waters
where I picked up this baton
floating up
from river bottom
braided silver and gold
adorned with black stones
snail shells
specks of starshine
all spelling my name

I crawled through the morass that
builds empire
waded through the quicksand
called commerce
outran the makers of new ways to own
freedom
and grabbed the staff
a road map to my very self

Balanced it on my head
carried it on my back
leaned on it as I
walked my beauty across the country
like Sonia Sanchez told me

birthed my blood child in poetry
like Octavia Butler showed me
spoke my home into reality
like Toni Morrison said it should be
swayed these hips like an offering
when Lucille Clifton set me free

Yes, I'm running with these words
spelled out by my
mothers
mothers
mothers
whispered into my mind
in the waters of the womb

We coming now, y'all
invisible
like the new moon

So mind the time
is in the mind
my mind is mine
free to be
I is we
is now
is ready to
wake up

Wake up

Know the cast of
characters
that castrate
the monoliths
malign our mates
kill our seeds
tossed across swaths of dry earth
consumed by birds of prey
interlopers

business brokers
broken men

You have been warned:
this ain't the end

Spirit Is

Spirit is more than a wisp of smoke or
philosophy
dusty doctrine
or what's trendy
it's the baby's smile
your first orgasm
a Frisbee flying over fields of green
it's birdsong
and tsunamis
rolling your waist to
Bob Marley
church bells electrifying
mamas in white doilies
it's an apology falling from your lovers lips
and an extra plate of
ackee and saltfish

Let My Love Be a Canvas

Let my love
be a canvas
where you paint
your reflection

Trapped

In my fourth decade
of life
I now know
I've been trapped
by my mother's fear
and can you blame her
for building this fortress
around us?

Locked in the fowl coop
for breaking a plate
lashed until the blood was let
for dirtying
the one good shoes
school days with
nose pressed up against
the window of a
whites-only ballet studio
built for those Kingston girls
from British Isles
exiled among the forgotten
faces of Akan, Ashanti, Twi

And she did not understand that
dem is We
even when chestnut hues
and freckles made their way into our skin
we too have oldest world kin,
you know?

"Well, Keisha...It's a white man's world. We just live in it..."

I hear you, mom
I love you for what you endured
to bring me here
but I create worlds
It's my job to dream

51

imagine
for those bred to be
blind
Love is my palette
I fear no man
I use this body like a chisel
a shovel
a machete
and I will never stop
until I am
the biggest
dream I
can imagine
because the prescience
wasn't beat out of me
and I have had enough food
and books
and the anonymity of
a big city
to remember
what you have been forced
to forget

Age

Age should
expand the iris
of your name
into a doorway
that lets the blazing
light,
splintered through
darkness,
come into clearer view
years should bloom
you like
a field of freesias
under the sun
of your mind
and unfurl you into
into one of the beautiful things
in time
your journey
in bone and skin
should mark
a firmly-trodden path
into clay
to make a way toward home
for those lost
in the thicket
we should not just grow up
but grow in
and study
the sound that
spawned the stars
we are uncoiling
toward the greatest
possibility of the
grandest idea
just to know
how fire exploded
from blackness

into a heartbeat
a grain of corn
an ocean tide
laughter
age is tempering us
into the perfect shape
of the
divine

Return Trippin'
A Meditation on Reincarnation

This time/life
has been an exercise
in remembering
the red bank rivers of Oyo
canopy of green
and electric earth
the running in the dark
and the bounty on my flesh
war
war
war
splitting us in two
the pieces of my mind
on pottery shards in old Calabar
cocooned in petroglyphs
I call doodles

The family,
generations of questions
and afflictions,
planted in places with saint names
doing the devil's work
the knowing of us selves
that we couldn't do
in daylight
hidden behind 'pet names'
and digging songs

And we came back
we come back
we are back
still asking
"Ain't I a Woman?"
I is
We am
always

She
a head full of
mermaids and pennies
words like
honey and giggles
spiraling on the wind

But still
in all the days
in all the ways
the ashes of these
racehorse lives
barb wire around my
memory
keep me safe from the
rage of running
the mazes
I built in my sleep

Yet,
I know you
I know us
All
rearranged
but still the same
loving and
not
in all the same ways

I think came here to
remember
so I could finally learn how
to forget

And then
pitch a hammock
among the stars
laugh at all the things
so small

so un-real
all me
and still
not
And just
for once
and for all
become
the perfect
I
who first
forgot

Everything is Necessary

every
thing
is necessary,
required to
be

is
just
is

how you see
is up to
you

are you
pink and green
caladium,
a field of hearts
in bloom,
bowing beneath
the rust/gold
gown of a
redwood tree?

or are
you
misery?

a spirit
cemented
to the stone
walls of its
temple,
crumbling and
crashing
onto
every mirror

that enters

forgetting
that all you are
is We,
a thousand-petal
flower
rocking
in the breeze called
time

the symphony of
lives
is merely
one second
one breath
to the great mind
dreaming these
colors
and every shape
that blooms
in galaxies

your mission is
to see
know that this is
one cradle
and we are an
infant with
infinite eyes
we are dancing
droplets
fallen from the sky
that speaks every
thing
into
a whirlpool
a black spool of
sound

that moves us
like the
ecstasy of
lovers becoming
one body
one melody

you are to
sing
until you have
no more breath
enjoy this vantage point
now

the only
death
is insisting
that your eyes stay shut
see clearly
before time's
up

About the Poet

Keisha-Gaye Anderson is a Jamaican-born poet, creative writer, visual artist, and media professional. She is the author of the poetry collection *Gathering the Waters* (Jamii Publishing 2014). Her writing has appeared in such publications as *Kweli Journal, Small Axe Salon, Renaissance Noire, Killens Review of Arts and Letters, Mosaic Literary Magazine, African Voices Magazine, Streetnotes: Cross Cultural Poetics, Caribbean in Transit Arts Journal, The Mom Egg Review,* and many others. She is a past participant of the VONA Voices and Callaloo Creative Writing workshops, and was a fellow at the North Country Institute for Writers of Color. Keisha has also been shortlisted for the Small Axe Literary Competition. She was selected as a 2018 Brooklyn Public Library Artist in Residence. Keisha holds an M.F.A. in creative writing from The City College, CUNY.

CPSIA information can be obtained
at www.ICGtesting.com
Printed in the USA
FFHW020750140619
52994900-58618FF